# Talons

## north american birds of prey

by
millie miller
and
cyndi nelson

## Johnson Books
Boulder

second printing 1990

**Imagine!** A hawk perched & waiting for the heat of the morning sun. Finally, on outstretched wings, he lets the rising thermals lift him, circling & soaring higher & higher until he vanishes from sight. Then he tucks his wings & begins to glide slowly down to earth until he reaches a neighboring thermal. He soars again, then glides & soars, working up an appetite for breakfast. **Suddenly,** he spies something move in the grass & dives. Tearing the air & hurtling at lightning speed, he hammers his talons like thunder into his prey! The mouse didn't stand a preyer!"

Eagles, hawks, falcons, ospreys & vultures are the day-time hunters or diurnal birds of prey. Lethal talons, hooked beaks & exceptional eyesight are all common to these majestic predators. They can easily capture creatures much larger than themselves but mostly feed on mice & small mammals, even insects.

Identification of raptors is tricky. Females tend to be larger. Immatures generally change a season or more before acquiring their adult feathers. Some species even come in different color forms... the same bird but with variations in plumage. Many mate for life, even in the same nest year after year. In times of plenty, they raise bigger families.

We apologize to the raptors we didn't have room for. Open skies to you... Harris, Gray, Roadside, Common Black, White-tailed & Zone-tailed Hawks (SW); Short-tailed Hawk (SE) & Crested Caracara (S). And good lift to all you Hang Gliders out there who share the thermals.

Increasing modernization & the resulting pollutants have had a damaging effect on birds of prey. If we serve as considerate caretakers of this jolly green planet, we will all soar a little higher. We can do it!

**Thunder in the Sky**

Owls & Ospreys have a reversible outer toe for an extra firm grip.

Osprey footpads have spicules for grasping slippery fish.

talons

Osprey

(window) wing panel

primaries

carpal patch

wrist

flight feathers

secondaries

(over the eye) supraorbital ridge

cere

superciliary line

gape

nape

mustache mark

streaking (vertical)

patagial mark

barring (horizontal)

undertail coverts

underwing coverts

terminal band

subterminal band

dark trailing edge on flight feathers

# Raptor Map

SUMMER
ALL YEAR
WINTER

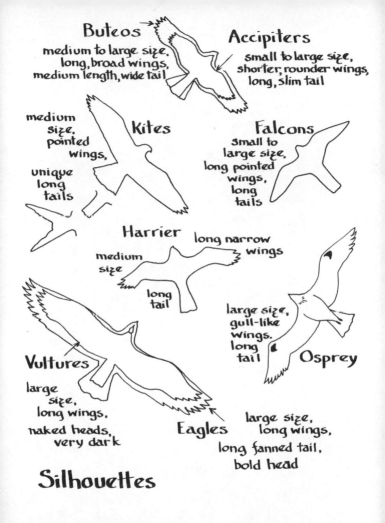

Buteos
medium to large size,
long, broad wings,
medium length, wide tail

Accipiters
small to large size,
shorter, rounder wings,
long, slim tail

Kites
medium size, pointed wings,
unique long tails

Falcons
Small to large size,
long pointed wings,
long tails

Harrier
medium size
long narrow wings
long tail

large size,
gull-like wings,
long tail
Osprey

Vultures
large size,
long wings,
naked heads,
very dark

Eagles
large size,
long wings,
long fanned tail,
bold head

Silhouettes

FEATURES... L 26"± WS 67"±

Large CARRION EATER resembling the "All American Turkey." DARK BROWN BODY has a naked RED HEAD. In flight, has contrasting DARK AND SILVERY UNDERWING feathers. LONG TAIL. SOARS for hours in wide circles, tilting "wobbley" & scanning. Dusky-headed immatures resemble adult Black Vulture. GLIDES in STRONG V. SLOW WING FLAPS & long glides differ from Black's rapid wing beats & short glides. HABITAT... Hangs out in dead trees, near roadsides & in OPEN COUNTRY. Roosts in trees, up to groups of 70. with wings spread to the sun, May sit waiting for morning thermals warm enough to soar on. No nest. Eggs usually laid on the ground, in caves or hollow stumps, often in swamps. Chicks fed by regurgitation. MORSELS... A rare sense of smell enables this unforgettable red head to locate hidden meals. Vultures, the strong silent type, only hiss & grunt. Their naked heads have no feathers to soil while gorging on rotten food. This reduces infection & makes their heads look tiny. Since "buzzards" usually do not hunt, they have weaker legs & feet, duller claws & bills.

**Turkey Vulture**  Cathartes aura

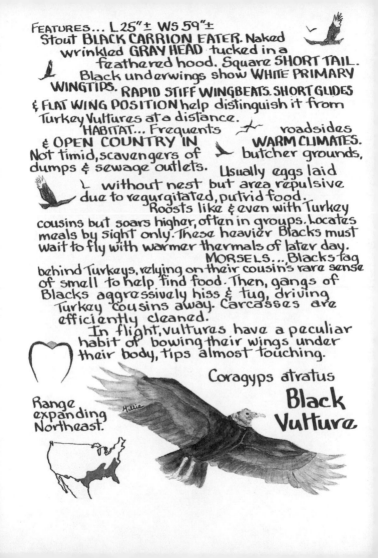

FEATURES... L 25"± WS 59"±

Stout BLACK CARRION EATER. Naked wrinkled GRAY HEAD tucked in a feathered hood. Square SHORT TAIL. Black underwings show WHITE PRIMARY WINGTIPS. RAPID STIFF WINGBEATS. SHORT GLIDES & FLAT WING POSITION help distinguish it from Turkey Vultures at a distance.

HABITAT... Frequents roadsides & OPEN COUNTRY IN WARM CLIMATES. Not timid, scavengers of butcher grounds, dumps & sewage outlets. Usually eggs laid without nest but area repulsive due to regurgitated, putrid food.

Roosts like & even with Turkey cousins but soars higher, often in groups. Locates meals by sight only. These heavier Blacks must wait to fly with warmer thermals of later day.

MORSELS... Blacks tag behind Turkeys, relying on their cousin's rare sense of smell to help find food. Then, gangs of Blacks aggressively hiss & tug, driving Turkey cousins away. Carcasses are efficiently cleaned.

In flight, vultures have a peculiar habit of bowing their wings under their body, tips almost touching.

*Coragyps atratus*

# Black Vulture

Range expanding Northeast.

FEATURES... L23"± WS 63"± Under wings
This large FISH EATER whitish with
has WHITE UNDER- BLACK
PARTS & wide BLACK CARPAL
EYE STRIPE. PATCH.
Immatures sim-
ilar but with white
edged upper feathers.
HABITAT... Only one
species, almost world
wide. FOUND NEAR
WATER, coastlines, lakes
& rivers. "Courtship dis-
play is magnificent!
Males perform a
fish dance, flying
up & down with
fish gripped in
talons, displaying to females
what great providers
they will be. "*
Huge stick nests
(weighing up to ½ ton
from yearly additions) in
tree or pole-like structure.
Uses shrill whistle,
"chewk, chewk, chewk"
to defend nest.

Soars
& GLIDES
GULL-LIKE
above the
water, diving
in talons
first...
sometimes
submerging
totally.

Lifts
from
surface
& points
fish head
forward before
shaking like a dog in midair.

MORSELS..."Fish Hawks"
are the only raptors having a
reversible outer toe like owls. In addition,
they have spiny spicules on bottoms of feet to help
catch & hold slippery fish. Dense compact feathers
repel water, & an enlarged cere can cover nostrils
under water. A powerful grip on too large a
fish can pull under & drown an Osprey.

Pandion
haliaetus

Osprey

*Trica Oshant - Hawk Mt.

FEATURES... L 22"± WS 51"± All black back has purplish hue. Lacks "fierce" bony ridge over red eyes. Immature has greenish cast on back, shorter tail (salad fork) & white tipped flight & tail feathers. HABITAT... Swamps & marshes of the Southeast & Gulf Coast. Hunts on the wing. Can pluck insects in mid-air, bending head to eat "hand-to-mouth." Also drinks in the air, swallow-like. Swaying high in the tree tops, loose but well-concealed nests of twigs are extravagantly lined with moss.

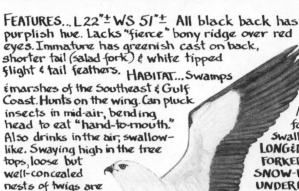

Named for its swallow-like, LONG & DEEPLY FORKED TAIL. SNOW-WHITE UNDERPARTS dramatic against BLACK TAIL & FLIGHT FEATHERS.

cyndi

Slow, limber wing beats and constantly scissoring tail create graceful aerial displays.

MORSELS... Easily recognized from a distance by their superb aerial ballet. A "social-kite," often flies & dines in groups, chatting "kii, ki, ki" as they go. Dips & dives, skimming the water to bathe.

A rare cousin, the Hook-billed Kite of the Texas Rio Grande Valley, also lacks a ridge over the eyes, is feathered more like a buteo, has paddle-shaped wings & uses its large hooked bill to eat tree snails.

*Elanoides forficatus*

# Swallow-tailed Kite

FEATURES...
WS 39"±
L 15"±

cyndi

Has gray back & primary flight feathers with white underwing coverts accented by a **BLACK CARPAL PATCH.** Often **HOVERS WITH LEGS DANGLING,** whistling..."keep, keep, keep."

Its **THOROUGHLY WHITE** appearance, seen from afar, earned its former name, White-tailed Kite. When perched, the upper wing coverts show off the **BLACK SHOULDER PATCH.** Immatures quickly outgrow their brownish cast & streaked breast. Perched, wing tips meet tail tip. Flight is light & gull-like with steady wing beats.

HABITAT...Gather in marshes & open country dotted with trees. At sunup & sundown, you can catch them hovering around the local meadow gulping down fast field mice. Occasionally hunt from a high perch. Dry grasses & roots line twig nests high in deciduous trees.

MORSELS...On a breezy spring day, children of all ages take to the meadow with paper & string to imitate this family of birds. Riding the wind, kites seem motionless in the sky. The last tally showed an increase of Black-shouldered kites, & though non-migratory, they are also enlarging their territories.

A rare Florida cousin, the Snail (or Everglade) kite, has paddle-shaped wings, floppy flight & a long, hooked beak for fresh water snail diet.

# Black-shouldered Kite

*Elanus caerulus*

Graceful & falcon-like in appearance. **OVERALL GRAY.** Whitish head, deep red eyes and **FLARED BLACK TAIL.**

Soar & glide gracefully for hours.

cyndi

FEATURES... L14"± WS31"± **OUTER PRIMARY MUCH SHORTER.** White tipped secondaries form whitish bar when perched. Immatures are brown with streaked underparts & underwing coverts. Their dark notched tails have three light bands. The teenagers (sub-adults) of this clan have a gray "bod" but flight & tail feathers are like immatures. Perched, pointed wing tips extend beyond tail tips.

HABITAT... Open woods and wet meadows from the Mississippi Valley east but starting to head west, young man. Hunt in flocks, feasting on a variety of insects snatched & eaten in mid-air. Flimsy nests, built in the top of the nearest high tree, are lined with green leaves. When disturbed near the nest, cries "phee-phew"... otherwise not much of a talker.

MORSELS... A social butterfly (leisurely flies & playfully somersaults with many fine-feathered friends) ... but has been known to pluck off the feet & wings of insects before gobbling up their tasty little bodies. Migrates & roosts in flocks of up to several hundred. Comes from Greek word "iktinos", meaning "a kite."

*Ictinia mississippiensis*

# Mississippi Kite

FEATURES... L 18"± WS 43"±
This slim "Marsh Hawk" is the only North American harrier.

Smaller **MALE...** **STEEL BLUE** above, white below with distinct black-tipped flight feathers. Hunts low, zig-zagging and harassing ("harrying") its prey on **V SHAPED WINGS.**

**DARK "HOODED" HEAD HAS OWL-LIKE FACE. WHITE RUMP PATCH, LONG WINGS & TAIL.** **FEMALE...** **BROWN** above with dark streaked underparts & barred flight feathers. Immatures also brown with solid rufous underparts. Perched, wing tips short of tail tip.

**HABITAT...** **MARSHES &** open fields. Dawn & dusk hunters, females favor mammals & the men folk are for birds. The male does great loops & dives to court his females. Well-hidden grass nests built on the ground. Dad hunts, passing prey to a mom mid-air (claw-to-claw or drop-catch), leaving her to nest while he tends to the rest of his wives. Generally quiet except for short whistles notifying food drops.

**MORSELS...**

Feathers around unusually large ear openings give the owl-like appearance & owl-like ability to hunt by sound. Perches close to or on the ground. Not to be confused with heavier Rough-legged Hawk that shares hunting areas.

*Circus cyaneus*
**Northern Harrier**

cyndi

FEATURES... L 11"± WS 23"±

North America's SMALLEST ACCIPITER has a THIN, SQUARE, WHITE-TIPPED TAIL & small ROUNDED HEAD with blue-gray crown & back. White underwing coverts and UNDERPARTS BARRED CINNAMON. Flight feathers are gray above & heavily barred below. Immatures are dark brown with rufous streaking on underparts.

Flight has LIGHT RAPID WING BEATS followed by glides... head barely extending beyond the "wrists" of the wings.

HABITAT... Accipiters are WOODLAND hawks, their short, rounded wings & long slim tails perfect for the reckless high-speed chase of forest prey.

Hunts from trees, almost exclusively EATING SMALL BIRDS plucked in mid-air or perched at feeders. Nests of twigs on low branches. Voice is a shrill "kik-kik-kik."

MORSELS... In Latin, Accipiter means "bird of prey." Perched, their wing tips reach halfway to tail tips. The Sharp-shinned is named for the sharp ridges on its "lower leg."

Accipiter striatus

# Sharp-shinned Hawk

FEATURES... L 17"± WS 31"± Easily confused with the Sharp-shinned. This **MEDIUM-SIZE** accipiter has a long **ROUNDED TAIL** ending with a wide white band. Has large **SQUARISH HEAD, DARK GRAY/BLUE CROWN** & lighter back. Resembling the Sharp-shinned, underparts & underwing coverts are white with **CINNAMON** barring, flight feathers are gray above & heavily barred below. Immatures are dark brown with rufous streaking on underparts.

In flight, Cooper's head extends beyond wrists & wing beats are stiffer.

MORSELS...When perched, raised hackles make Cooper a real block head. This "chicken hawk" is the size of a crow.

HABITAT...
**WOODLANDS** with open areas. Ambushes birds & small mammals from a hidden perch. Shallow stick nest built mostly by the dad, vigorously defended with harsh "kak-kak-kak."

Accipiters are all red-eyed. Flight is "flap-flap-glide". Camouflaged by their woodland lifestyle.

Females are much larger.

Accipiter cooperii
# Cooper's Hawk

FEATURES... L 21"± WS 41"±
    LARGEST of North American accipiters. GRAY with a dark head & thick WHITE EYE STRIPE. Back is slate gray, tail is faintly banded & wedge shaped. Pale gray underparts & underwings are softly mottled with black. Flight feathers are lightly banded below.
    Under-tail coverts are white & fluffy. Young are paler brown than other accipiters but head has the white eye line. Soaring on level wings like a buteo, its flight has strong, stiff wing beats followed by glides.

        HABITAT... NORTHERN & MOUNTAIN FORESTS.
        Mates for life. Larger than a crow, hunts from perch or while flying. Preys mostly on medium to large birds (jays, grouse, small hawks) & mammals (chipmunks, squirrels, rabbits).
        Male builds bulky platform nest in a tall tree which some years is rebuilt by female.

Eggs are vigorously defended by sharp screams & blunt attacks.

        MORSELS... Goshawk is derived from the European "goose-hawk."

Relentlessly pursues prey through heavy woods.

Wings are long for an accipiter.

Accipiter gentilis
# Goshawk

Millie

FEATURES...L 17"± WS 40"± A RED-SHOULDERED buteo with distinct **WING WINDOWS** at base of primaries on all four color forms.

This crescent-shaped wing mark can be seen from above or below. Flight feathers heavily barred, appearing almost checkered from above. **BLACK TAIL WITH NARROW WHITE BANDS.** Perched, wing tips short of tail tip.

Head & back are brown.

Rufous underparts & underwing coverts. Immatures similar but paler with streaked underparts. Flies with quick, stiff wing beats, glides on bowed wings, soars on flat wings but does not hover.

HABITAT...Prefers wet lowland woods near farms. Also at home in suburban neighborhoods. Sits quietly on low perch, scouting for small mammals, birds, reptiles, fish and insects. Their courtship scream "kee-yar" is often imitated by blue-jays. Builds a platform nest of sticks in a high tree crotch.

MORSELS... A <u>California form</u> has the reddest shoulder patch & rufous underparts. A <u>Texas form</u> is paler, while a <u>Florida form</u> is also pale with a gray head. All immature forms are more heavily barred. These varieties tend to use high, more exposed perches.

*Buteo lineatus*
# Red-Shouldered Hawk

**HABITAT...** A quiet, mild-mannered hawk of the deciduous woodlands. Often perched watching for small mammals, reptiles & large insects. Nests, built loosely with twigs close to tree trunk, are only used once. Occasionally redecorates an old crow's or squirrel's nest. "Pweeeee" whistle is earpiercing.

**FEATURES...** L 15"± WS 34"±

**WHITE UNDERWINGS** edged with black are slightly pointed.

Immatures have malar stripe, more noticeable streaks on head & breast, a square white window panel on underwing flight feathers & narrower tail bands.

Young Red-Shouldered & Red-tailed cousins resemble these immatures.

**Dark brown body** has rufous barred underparts.

The rarer dark form is... darker!! but keeps its banded tail. Perched, wing tips short of tail tip. Flies with quick, stiff wing beats, soars on flat wings but does not hover. **MORSELS...** A hawk watcher's delight is spotting a "kettle" of migrating Broad-wings... a large group of up to 5,000. Spiraling together in thermals, then flying in close formation between updrafts, threading "buteoful" floating streamers through the sky.

**Smallest, chunkiest buteo** & only one with **BOLD BLACK & WHITE BANDS ON TAIL.**

cyndi

*Buteo platypterus*

# Broad-winged Hawk

**FEATURES...** **L19"± WS51"±** Large slender buteo of the western plains with pointed wings & 3 color forms. The common <u>light form adult</u> has **WIDE BROWN BREAST BIB** under a **WHITE THROAT**. White underbelly & **UNDER-WING COVERTS CONTRAST WITH DARK FLIGHT FEATHERS.** Immature has buffy throat, streaked breast & less contrasting underwings. The rare <u>dark form</u> is sooty with rufous belly & underwing coverts. Undertail coverts noticeably light. <u>Rufous form</u> similar with barred undertail coverts. All fly with wings in V shape. Often soar and "kite."

**HABITAT...** At home on the range, PRAIRIES & meadows. Lallygag on trees & fence posts, watching for prey. Also hunt on the wing, sometimes following tractors in search of insects & unearthed rodents. Stick nest built on cliffs, yucca or lone tree. Remodeled yearly. Has plaintive note "kreeee" in flight or perched.

**MORSELS...** Migrate in flocks of several thousand. Sometimes descend as a cloud and scamper after grasshoppers. Ambush **GROUND SQUIRRELS** from their own hillocks. Can fly through the air, catching & eating **INSECTS** or bats with the greatest of ease.

Perched, wing tips reach tail tip.

Adult light form

*Buteo swainsoni*

# Swainson's Hawk

FEATURES...
WS 47"±
L 19"±

cyndi

"When all else fails, call it a Red-tail." Most common & widespread buteo has many individual variations. Luckily, most have REDDISH TAILS. More common Eastern form usually has broad DARK STREAKED BAND ACROSS WHITE BELLY. Western dark form has SOLID DARK BROWN BODY with RUFOUS BANDED TAIL. Western light form has WIDER, DARKER BELLY BAND & RICHER RUFOUS color. Western rufous form has DARK CHOCOLATE BELLY BAND on deep rufous body & RUFOUS BANDED TAIL.

All immatures are generally more mottled with grayish tails. In the SW, the Fuertes' is like darker Eastern adult with no belly band. On the northern plains, the Krider's is similar to Eastern but whiter head & tail with no belly band. On southern plains, the Harlan's is coal black with streaked breast & 4 tail variations. Perched, adult Western, Fuertes' & Harlan's wing tips meet tail tip... others, shorter. All have steady wing beats, slow & deep. Glide with wings in slight V, hover & kite, but soaring is their cup of tea.

HABITAT... Often perched at wood's edge. Hunts open & forest areas for mice, small mammals & insects. Stick nests lined with tender roots & twigs. MORSELS... Loud wheezing "kree-e-e" squeal.

Phenomenal eyesight... can spot a meadow mouse from 100'& then comes the power dive. Covorting antics of courtship begin years of togetherness. Important in rodent control.

Buteo jamaicensis
**Red-tailed Hawk**

FEATURES... L 23"± WS 56"± Immatures have whitish
leggins. Rarer <u>dark form</u> is deep rufous with silvery
flight feathers & tail.

Has slow, strong wing beats, glides with wings in V
in great circles but often hunts close to the ground or from
a fence post. HABITAT... A western "squirrel hawk" of
**BRUSHY PRAIRIES**, open plains & barren badlands. Huge nests
in trees, cliffs or even haystacks are made of sticks lined with
dried cow chips, turf or roots. Alarm note of "kree-a."

MORSELS... Ferruginous means the color of
iron rust. Fierce & strong enough to scare coyotes
away from nest. Resembles the Golden Eagle
in feathered leggins, flight, nest & diet.

soars high

Sometimes hunt in pairs, pouncing on GROUND SQUIRRELS & prairie dogs, eating enough to be effective exterminators for farmers.

In flight, RUFOUS LEGS FORM V AGAINST ALL WHITE BELLY & TAIL.

The largest of buteos, has legs feathered
to the toes. The <u>light form</u>'s head is
large & whitish. Tail has no bands.

Perched, wing tips close to tail tip.

Buteo regalis
Ferruginous Hawk

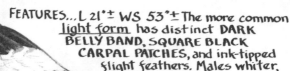

FEATURES... L 21"± WS 53"± The more common <u>light form</u> has distinct DARK BELLY BAND, SQUARE BLACK CARPAL PATCHES, and ink-tipped flight feathers. Males whiter, females browner. Immatures brown but less streaked. Perched, wing tips meet tail tip.

cyndi

HABITAT... OPEN FIELDS & meadows, perching on low limbs to watch for prey. Hunts at dusk for lemmings, mice & other mammals. Deep twig nests on tundra cliffs or tree tops are moss lined to insulate eggs against the Arctic cold. Alternates the same nests over many years. Called "squalling hawk" by the Eskimos because of mews & cries. MORSELS... Unusually mellow due to rare human contact. Many have a unique white & black bull's eye on the nape of necks.

Often seen HOVERING, this large buteo has two color forms, both with an obvious BROAD BLACK TERMINAL TAIL BAND & legs feathered to toes.

Flies with slow wing beats & low glides, often in a slight V.

# Rough-legged Hawk   Buteo lagopus

FEATURES...L 31"± WS 7'± It takes 4 to 5 years & 5 different plumages for this American emblem to mature to its "dollar" form. The immature form is dark all over, resembling a Golden Eagle except LEGS FEATHERED HALFWAY. They then molt through 2 stages of whiter bellies, back & head. The final transition keeps a dark eye line, adds more white on tail & develops yellowing eyes, beak & cere. The adult, our familiar national bird, regains a dark brown body & completes the MAJESTIC WHITE TAIL & HEAD with piercing YELLOW EYES & STRONG BEAK. Slow powerful wing beats. Soars on flat wings, often with other Baldies.

HABITAT...FOUND WHERE THE FISHING IS GOOD, they also attack water fowl & frequently pirate meals from other fisher-birds. Dead fish & carrion are "easy pickings." Mating for life, the couple makes yearly additions to nest, sometimes ending up with a thousand-pound mansion with a water-front view. Chatter to each other in thin, soft "kak, kak, kak" voices.

MORSELS...A social bird, often roosts & perches in groups. Enormous tree-top nests sometimes topple in a windstorm. "Balde", in Old English means white.

*Haliaeetus leucocephalus*

## Bald Eagle

Millie

FEATURES... L30"± WS 7'± Large brown eagle with majestic GOLDEN CROWN & NAPE OF NECK. The immature, taking 4 years & 2 moltings to mature, is brown with dark eyes. Its tail has a white base ending in a wide dark band. Subadult adds more brown to the tail. Adult tail retains faint gray bands, the eyes are now yellow & the strong BEAK HAS A BLACK TIP. LEGS FEATHERED TO TOES. Flies with strong, slow wing beats. Soars with wings in slight V & glides with wing tips up. Daredevil dives up to 200 mph.

HABITAT... Mountain hideaways, canyons & remote rangelands. Helps keep rabbit population in check but also eats carrion & mammals as large as antelope & deer. Graceful & nimble for its size, can also nab a variety of fowl. Sometimes hunts with a lifetime mate. Alternates yearly through several huge nests (up to 10' across & 4' deep), built mainly on cliffs, in trees or on phone poles. Quiet with occasional "kya, kya."

Some power towers have nesting platforms built in to protect nests from high winds.

MORSELS... Around the world, some power companies install devices on utility poles to protect eagles from zapping themselves on the wires during landings.

Aquila chrysaetos

# Golden Eagle

FEATURES...L10"± WS 22"± The early settlers really misnamed this one. Still known as the SPARROW HAWK, this is the most common <u>falcon</u> in North America & doesn't eat many sparrows at all. A good looker, the only small falcon with RUFOUS BACK & TAIL. Head is handsomely marked with white cheeks, BLACK WHISKERS & crowned with gray.

The ladies' ensemble includes toffee-streaked bodice with matching wings and delicately multi-banded tail.

Perched, wing tips reach well past middle of tail. Soars with fanned tail and hunts regularly while hovering or kiting.

HABITAT...Well-adapted to prairie, desert or city life. Dines primarily on insects but will lunch on rodents & reptiles. Prefab nests are holes in trees, cactus, cliffs or buildings. Some people help them out by putting up kestrel boxes. Their frequent noisy cry is "killy, killy, killy."

MORSELS...When in a dither, the falcon family like to bob their heads & flick their tails.

The gentlemen sport blue-gray wings, rufous vests & black-tipped tails. The lads have black & white striped vests & completely barred rufous backs.

Often seen atop road-side fence posts & utility wires.

Falco sparverius
## American Kestrel

FEATURES... L 11"± WS 24"± Some-times called the pigeon hawk, this small "wizard" has three color forms, all LACKING THE BOLD FALCON MUSTACHE. The TAIGAS & BLACK FORMS HAVE DARK UNDERWINGS.
<u>Male Taigas</u> have slate blue crown, back & tail bands. Females and immatures have brown backs & buffy tail bands. The <u>Black form</u> is basic black... no pearls. Flies with rapid, strong wing beats, often low & in direct pursuit.

The larger <u>Prairie form</u> is paler with wider tail bands.

HABITAT... Nests in open meadows or coniferous forests. They birdwatch from a perch, ready to startle entire flocks & snag the stragglers with "magical" maneuvers. Also eat rodents & "flying dragons." Rusty eggs laid on ground or in abandoned tree nests.

Quiet except for a rapid "ki-ki-ki-kee" alarm call. Perched, wing tips short of tail tip.

MORSELS... Mimics the flight of a pigeon to sneak up on unwary prey. Noble ladies preferred to hunt with this trusting & easily trained falcon because of its small size, returning it to the wild after a season.

Millie

Taiga

# Merlin
*Falco columbarius*

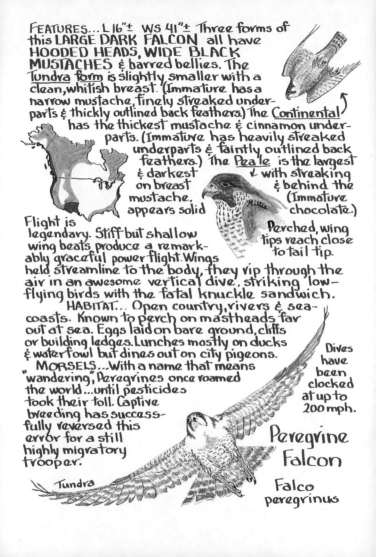

FEATURES... L 16"± WS 41"± Three forms of this LARGE DARK FALCON all have HOODED HEADS, WIDE BLACK MUSTACHES & barred bellies. The <u>Tundra</u> form is slightly smaller with a clean, whitish breast. (Immature has a narrow mustache, finely streaked underparts & thickly outlined back feathers.) The <u>Continental</u> has the thickest mustache & cinnamon underparts. (Immature has heavily streaked underparts & faintly outlined back feathers.) The <u>Peale</u> is the largest & darkest on breast mustache, appears solid with streaking & behind the (Immature chocolate.)

Perched, wing tips reach close to tail tip.

Flight is legendary. Stiff but shallow wing beats produce a remarkably graceful power flight. Wings held streamline to the body, they rip through the air in an awesome vertical dive, striking low-flying birds with the fatal knuckle sandwich.

HABITAT... Open country, rivers & seacoasts. Known to perch on mastheads far out at sea. Eggs laid on bare ground, cliffs or building ledges. Lunches mostly on ducks & waterfowl but dines out on city pigeons.

MORSELS... With a name that means "wandering," Peregrines once roamed the world...until pesticides took their toll. Captive breeding has successfully reversed this error for a still highly migratory trooper.

Tundra

Dives have been clocked at up to 200 mph.

Peregrine Falcon

Falco peregrinus

FEATURES... L 22"± WS 48"± This majestic bird, largest of all falcons, has three color forms. The striking, common <u>White form</u> has DAZZLING WHITE underparts & the regal back of a snow leopard. The Gray <u>form</u> has gray back, white spotted underparts & TWO-TONED UNDERWINGS. The <u>Dark form</u> has DARK HOODED HEAD, light streaks on a dark belly & spotted underwing coverts. Immatures are like each adult form but have brown back feathers outlined in white & heavily streaked underparts. Perched, wing tips reach more than halfway to tailtip. Powerful wing beats are slow & deep but produce an amazingly rapid flight.

Dark

EXTREME WINTER

Near nest, cackles "kak-kak-kak."

HABITAT... This polar bird soars the ARCTIC TUNDRA, looking for favored ptarmigan or ducks & Arctic hare. Winters near the coast & prefers cliff ledges for nesting.

MORSELS... Belly feathers long enough to keep their toes warm. In olden days, a knightly gift of falconry.

Name is thought to come from "slang" Latin meaning "sacred" falcon

Millie

**Gyrfalcon**

*Falco rusticolus*

Gray

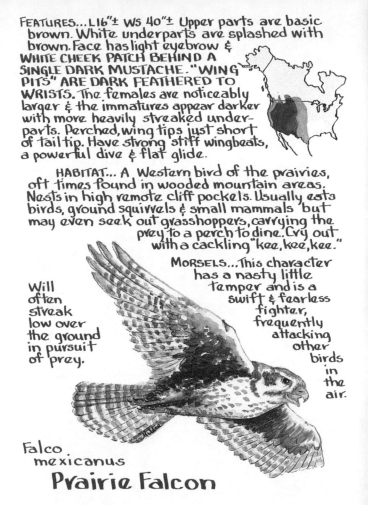

FEATURES... L 16"± WS 40"± Upper parts are basic brown. White underparts are splashed with brown. Face has light eyebrow & **WHITE CHEEK PATCH BEHIND A SINGLE DARK MUSTACHE. "WING PITS" ARE DARK FEATHERED TO WRISTS.** The females are noticeably larger & the immatures appear darker with more heavily streaked underparts. Perched, wing tips just short of tail tip. Have strong stiff wingbeats, a powerful dive & flat glide.

HABITAT... A Western bird of the prairies, oft times found in wooded mountain areas. Nests in high remote cliff pockets. Usually eats birds, ground squirrels & small mammals but may even seek out grasshoppers, carrying the prey to a perch to dine. Cry out with a cackling "kee, kee, kee."

MORSELS... This character has a nasty little temper and is a swift & fearless fighter, frequently attacking other birds in the air.

Will often streak low over the ground in pursuit of prey.

Falco mexicanus
# Prairie Falcon

Most owls are creatures of the night.

Their eyes are huge & like humans, they have binocular vision... because the eyes point straight ahead, they can see the same thing with both eyes at the same time thus greatly increasing their visual acuity. However, the eyes are fixed in the sockets so owls must rotate their heads (up to 270°) to look around.

Barn

Screech

Hawk

Elf

Saw-whet

Great Horned

Long-eared

Barred

Great Gray

W h o o o o o o o o o o

Snowy

Short-eared

Burrowing

gives a HOOT!

More rod cells in their eyes make maximum night vision possible. Fewer cone cells leave them essentially colorblind, seeing only shades of gray.

Extraordinary hearing also helps them to locate prey in the dark of night. Owls can hear a mouse step on a twig up to 75' away or detect a lemming burrowing under the snow. Large ear openings hidden behind facial discs may be different in placement & size, helping to pinpoint the direction & distance of a sound.

Facial discs aren't just horn-rimmed glasses but help to funnel sounds into the ear openings. "Ear tufts" are only fancy feathers & should not be confused with the real thing. "Egyptian head movements" fine-tune their eye & ear acuity.

Owls have another remarkable adaptation for night stalking. Fluffy edges on their flight feathers enable them to fly on silent wings. This calm allows the owl to listen "unruffled" while flying & seize their prey without warning.

During the day, an owl can sit unnoticed on a tree branch, boldly upright & close to the trunk, hidden by its bark-like coloration. Flocks of birds often harass a roosting owl, a good tip to its whereabouts.

Pellets are another clue. These regurgitated undigestable parts of their diet are sometimes piled at the bottom of their roosting trees. Knowing owl calls & silhouettes can help locate owls as well.

Owls have four talons on each foot...the outer talon can be rotated backward for a better grasp. Female owls are usually larger & lay more eggs when there is more food. As a bird of prey, the owl is helpful in rodent control...and its only predator ...is man...

**FEATURES...** L 9"± WS 21"±
A common **SMALL NOCTURNAL OWL** of the east. Well-camouflaged in both the mottled gray & red forms. **SMALL WIDE SET EAR TUFTS,** yellow eyes & streaked underparts. Fast and steady wing beats.
**HABITAT...** Woodlands, orchards & backyard groves.

Roosts & lays eggs in natural tree cavities.

Diversified diet of small mammals, reptiles, birds, fish & worms. Call is less a screech than a **QUIVERING WHISTLE DOWN THE SCALE.**

**MORSELS...**
This quiet, gentle owl has western cousins... all with small ear tufts in gray & red forms. The larger <u>kennicotti</u> (N.W. coast) has fine bars on underparts. Likes an Eastern diet. Sounds like a bouncing ball. The spotted <u>Trichopsis</u> (Arizona) is smaller, whiskered & has bolder bars on belly. Eats mostly insects. Calls are a variation of "boot, boot, boot...boot." The <u>Flammeolus</u> (Rocky Mts. westward) is rare & the smallest Otus... the only small owl in N. America with dark eyes. Also prefers insects.

Male call is a steady mellow "hoo-HOO", often filling a moonlit night.

*Otus asio*

# Screech Owl (Eastern)

cyndi

FEATURES... L 22"± WS 56"± Large, well-known owl has **WHITE BIB** under its great head. **EAR TUFTS ARE WIDE SET** & forehead feathers are foreboding. Brownish underparts barred. Flight is heavy but graceful & swift, seldom above tree tops though may briefly soar to great heights. Occasional high perch shows its silhouette against the night sky. HABITAT... Wide range from woodlands to deserts to city parks. Aggressive, bloodthirsty hunter by day or night. Known to "kill" duck decoys. In times of plenty, will eat only choice tidbits of a large variety of prey but prefers rats & mice. Takes over abandoned hawk nests in trees or cliffs. Usually breeds before snow melt. Thick down aids winter incubation. Resonant "Whoo! whoo-whoo-whoo! Whoo! Whoo!" can be heard like a foghorn miles out at sea.

MORSELS... Gentle in their courtship but attack intruders viciously. Overly generous in variety & amount fed to owlets. Body & nest may smell of skunk. Each owl has distinct voice & responds to imitation calls.
Scientific name is for the state where it was first collected.

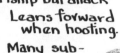

Leans forward when hooting.

Many sub-species.

*Bubo virginianus*
# Great Horned Owl

Millie

FEATURES... L14"± WS 39"±
SLENDER medium-sized grayish owl. Large dark **EARTUFTS ARE CLOSE TOGETHER** over rusty facial discs. Underside streaked. Long wings give large appearance in flight but has the grace & lightness of a butterfly.

HABITAT... A real "fly-by-night" owl. Swoops silently down on unsuspecting mice near woodland edges. Uses deserted squirrel's or crow's nests. Roosts unnoticed during the day, camouflaged by feathers near tree trunk. Has quiet, dove-like "hoo-hoo-hoo."

MORSELS... Seldom seen because so **NOCTURNAL. QUIET & WELL-HIDDEN** during the day. When frightened, stretches out long & thin. Fierce in defending young & has a great "wounded-bird act" to draw intruders away.

Fly with eartufts flat against their heads. Related Great Horned cousin is larger, has barred belly & ear tufts are farther apart.

Millie

*Asio otus*

# Long-eared Owl

FEATURES... L 15"± WS 41"±

How short are this owl's ears? If you ever see them... get measurements!

A tawny, medium-sized owl with ROUND HEAD, buffy facial discs & white eyebrows. PIERCING YELLOW EYES SURROUNDED BY BLACK FEATHERS. Undersides streaked with brown. DARK CARPAL PATCHES noticeable during FLAPPING, IRREGULAR FLIGHT.

HABITAT... DAYTIME OWL. Hunts low over marshes, prairies & tundra for mice & other small rodents in every continent except Australia.

Roosts & nests ON THE GROUND! Barks "keeyow" near the nest. Does a terrific "broken wing act" to divert attention. Courtship display is highlighted with 15-20 "toot-toot-tootings" & underbody wing-clapping.

MORSELS... Extremely adept at head rotation. Also comes in rare gray form. Similar to Long-eared Owl "whooo" however, nests in trees and hunts by night.

*Asio flammeus*

Short-eared Owl

FEATURES... L 17"± WS 45"± White, HEART-SHAPED FACE with small DARK EYES. A sleek owl with a tan back & WHITE FRECKLED BELLY. Stands knock-kneed on LONG LEGS. Similar orange form has golden belly. Flight is silent, swift & buoyant.

HABITAT... Widespread (except in coniferous mountains) but uncommon. Lives are shaped by "mice & men". Help control rodents by hunting open fields, farmlands & meadows. Once lived only in caves & hollow trees, now commonly housed in barns, attics & other man-made structures.

Calls are a hair-raising screech, a snore or a rasping "hiss".

MORSELS...
This monkey-faced owl can hunt by sound only, usually in the dead of night. Sleeps so soundly by day that it's hard to arouse & is dazed by bright light.

Builds no nests.

When threatened, does an aggressive "toe-dusting", moving head back and forth over talons.

cyndi

**BarnOwl** Tyto alba

FEATURES... L 24"± WS 61"± **LARGE ARCTIC GROUND OWL.**
**MOSTLY WHITE** with brown flecks. Yellow **eyes.** Females
& immatures are darker.
Legs feathered to the toes.
Strong direct flight, scanning ground as it glides.
HABITAT...Circumpolar.
Tundra during the summer.
In the winter, migrates short
distances to lower prairies,
fields, marshes & beaches.
Nests in grass-lined hollows on the
tundra. Prefers the twilight hunts
but forced into the daylight by
the summer's midnight sun.
Likes lemmings & mice but in
lean years, makes do with other
mammals, birds & fish.

Usually silent
except on breeding
grounds when gives a booming
"Whoo-whoo-whoo-whoo" far
over the tundra. Also whistles
& "barks" an alarm.
MORSELS...
Very solitary. Feathered
feet act as "snowshoes" &
insulation. Cyclic migrations
every 4 or 5 years bring
them far south as lemming
populations
wax and
wane.

**Snowy Owl**
Nyctea scandiaca

FEATURES... L 29"± WS 56'± The GIANT of N. Am. owls. LARGE RINGED FACIAL DISCS, NO EAR TUFTS & YELLOW EYES. Has prominent BLACK CHIN with a WHITE "BOWTIE". Belly is streaked gray, tail is long & legs are feathered to toes. Flies in spurts, low & slow. HABITAT... Boreal forests & high elevation pine & spruce. Eats small mammals. Lays smallish eggs in deserted nests. Call is a booming "Whoo-ooo-ooo." MORSELS... This cold land cousin of Barred and Spotted Owls actually has small body... its bulk is mainly feathers.

**Great Gray Owl**

*Strix nebulosa*

FEATURES... L 20"± WS 44"± Common gray-brown owl with LARGE ROUND HEAD. BROWN EYES set in large facial discs. BARRED "C-OWL" around neck & STREAKED BELLY. Flies high & silently with slow, heavy wing beats. HABITAT... Eastern deep moist woods & swamps. Hunts mostly by night, usually for mice. Also eats fish, birds, reptiles & insects. Lays eggs in tree cavities or abandoned nests. Heard night or day, squalling or barking but best known for "Who cooks for you? Who cooks for you-all?" MORSELS... Rare western cousin, the Spotted Owl, has BARRED UNDERPARTS, dark eyes & is heard in dense woods giving 3 or 4 hoots

**Barred Owl**

*Strix varia*

*Surnia ulula*

# Hawk Owl

**FEATURES...** L16"± WS 33"± This slim brown **HAWK-LIKE** owl has white spotted back & **BARRED BELLY.** Whitish facial discs rimmed with **BLACK EYEBROWS, SIDEBURNS & CHIN.** Has **LONG, BANDED TAIL** & short wings. Hawk-like flight is low & swift.

**HABITAT...** Boreal forests & brushy tundra. The most active **DAYTIME OWL,** hunting with the midnight sun. Perches on exposed tree tops watching for rodents or birds in winter. Lays eggs in tree cavities or abandoned nests. "Ki-ki-ki-ki" sounds like a hawk's cry.

**MORSELS...** Rarely seen.

HAWK

BURROWING

**FEATURES...** L10"± WS 22"±
Small, **SANDY-BROWN** owl with **LONG LEGS** and **SHORT TAIL.** Speckled round head has white eyebrows. Wears a dark collar on a white throat. Back is spotted, **UNDERSIDE BARRED.** Labored undulating flight close to ground. Often hovers.

**HABITAT...** A **GROUND OWL** of plains, deserts & open spaces—Sometimes does its own digging but usually nests in abandoned burrows. Lines nest with feathers, dried dung & remains of old prey. Hunts mostly at dusk & throughout the night for insects, rodents & reptiles. Common call is tremulous chattering or dove-like "coo-coo-hoo." **MORSELS...** May live in colonies in the West. Often **BOBS UP & DOWN** atop mounded entrance to burrow.

*Athene cunicularia*

# Burrowing Owl

Millie

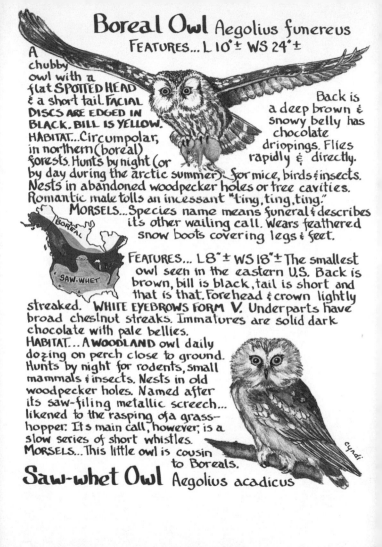

# Boreal Owl *Aegolius funereus*
## FEATURES... L 10"± WS 24"±

A chubby owl with a flat SPOTTED HEAD & a short tail. FACIAL DISCS ARE EDGED IN BLACK. BILL IS YELLOW. HABITAT... Circumpolar, in northern (boreal) forests. Hunts by night (or by day during the arctic summer) for mice, birds & insects. Nests in abandoned woodpecker holes or tree cavities. Romantic male tolls an incessant "ting, ting, ting."

Back is a deep brown & snowy belly has chocolate drippings. Flies rapidly & directly.

MORSELS... Species name means funeral & describes it's other wailing call. Wears feathered snow boots covering legs & feet.

FEATURES... L 8"± WS 18"± The smallest owl seen in the eastern U.S. Back is brown, bill is black, tail is short and that is that. Forehead & crown lightly streaked. WHITE EYEBROWS FORM V. Underparts have broad chestnut streaks. Immatures are solid dark chocolate with pale bellies.

HABITAT... A WOODLAND owl daily dozing on perch close to ground. Hunts by night for rodents, small mammals & insects. Nests in old woodpecker holes. Named after its saw-filing metallic screech... likened to the rasping of a grasshopper. Its main call, however, is a slow series of short whistles.

MORSELS... This little owl is cousin to Boreals.

# Saw-whet Owl *Aegolius acadicus*

cyndi

# Pygmy Owl

**Glaucidium gnoma**

FEATURES... L 7"± WS 15"± Tiny, brownish & bird-like. SPECKLED HEAD & shoulders. DARK STREAKS ON WHITE BELLY. "EYE-PATCHES" on BACK OF HEAD. LONG BARRED TAIL. Low, undulating flight. HABITAT... MOUNTAINOUS FORESTS near clearings. May hunt by day for mice & insects. Mellow whistle or dove-like "hoo" in breeding season. Nests in tree holes.

MORSELS... When perched, TAIL ANGLES TO SIDE. Size not to be confused with it's ferocity. Has 4 sub-species.

# Ferruginous Owl

**Glaucidium brasilianum**

FEATURES... L 7"± WS 15"± Rarer Pygmy cousin. Also has "EYE-PATCHES", SOLID RUSTY BACK & TAIL BARRED WITH BLACK. HEAD & FRONT STREAKED WITH RUST. Also has gray form. Flight similar. HABITAT... SAGUARO DESERTS of so. Arizona & lower Rio Grande Valley, Texas. Fierce hunter of lizards, insects & birds... sometimes larger than self. Nests in tree or cactus holes. Long rapid series of "churrups." MORSELS... Jerks & flips tail. Often attacked by flocks of birds.

# Elf Owl

**Micrathene whitneyi** FEATURES... L 5"± WS 15"± The TINIEST OWL in the world. Common gray form has buffy spots on back & head. Brown form has darker back. Both have SHORT TAIL, WHITE EYEBROWS & buffy cinnamon striped underparts. Rapid wing beats. HABITAT... SAGUARO DESERTS & wooded canyons. Hunts by night, catching large insects in talons.

Nests exclusively in deserted woodpecker holes, especially in saguaros. Mates whistle duet of descending "chewk, chewk, chewk" like a yipping puppy. MORSELS... Hides in saguaro holes by day, shielding its conspicuous eyes with a wing.

PYGMY

ELF

FERRUGINOUS

our thanks...
to all the folks &
foundations befriending
birds of prey...

especially to

**Trica Oshant**
of Hawk Mountain, Pa.
whose raptor savvy &
advice helped to give
this little book wings!

Dedication... to the

California Condor
L 46"± WS 109"±

Much larger
than an eagle,
these giant
vultures

have sometimes been
mistaken for low flying
aircraft. Eating carrion
exclusively, they have been
cleaning up the countryside
since prehistoric times.
Because of over population,
careless hunting, predator
poisonings & dwindling
ranges, only a handful
remain in a small mountain
area of southern California.
¡Qué lástima!

references...

**Clark**, William S. & Brian
K. Wheeler. _A Field Guide to
Hawks_. Boston: Houghton
Mifflin Co., 1987.

**Heintzelman**, Donald S.
_Guide to Owl Watching_.
Hermosa Beach, Calif. :
Winchester Publishing, 1984.

**Peterson**, Roger Tory.
_A Field Guide to Western
Birds_. Boston: Houghton
Mifflin Co., 1961.

**Robbins**, Chandler S.,
Bertel Bruun & Herbert
S. Zim. _A Guide to Field
Identification - Birds of
North America_. New York:
Golden Press, 1966.

**Terres**, John K.. _Audubon
Society Encyclopedia of
North American Birds_.
New York: Alfred A. Knopf,
Inc., 1980.

**Udvardy**, Miklos D.F..
_The Audubon Society
Field Guide to North
American Birds_. New
York: Alfred A. Knopf,
Inc., 1977.